Single Serving Vegetarian Recipes

To Soothe Arthritis

Polly Fielding

Copyright © 2018 Polly Fielding

All rights reserved.

ISBN-13: 978-1981942688

ISBN-10: 1981942688

Also by Polly Fielding

Single Serving Recipes To Soothe Arthritis

Delicious Diabetic Vegetarian Meals For One

The 5:2 Diet Made eZy

The 5:2 Vegetarian Diet Made eZy

Everything You Need For The 5:2 Diet (*co-authored with Emily Hanson & Lucy Lonsdale*)

Mindfulness For The 5:2 Diet

Moments Of Mindfulness

Time For Mindfulness

Nurturing Compassion

A Veritable Smorgasbord

Missing Factor

Going In Seine

Breaking The Silence

Letting Go (a trilogy comprising the three books below)

And This Is My Adopted Daughter

A Mind To Be Free

Crossing The Borderline

www.pollyfielding.com

To the memory of my mother, Mary Lewis, with love

CONTENTS

Introduction	1
Understanding Arthritis	3
Breakfasts	9
Index of Breakfasts	10
Lunches	38
Index of Lunches	39
Dinners	75
Index of Dinners	76

Acknowledgement

My grateful thanks to Sarah Reed, nutritionist, for her advice and encouragement

Introduction

Arthritis is such a widespread condition that all of us, if not directly affected by it, inevitably knows somebody who is.

And it can have an enormous impact on a person living with the disease, affecting not only their mobility but also their mood and social life.

However, it's important to know, if you have arthritis, that there are various positive changes you can make to your lifestyle that can alleviate its painful symptoms.

My mother developed rheumatoid arthritis at the age of thirty-three, which caused acute pain for the rest of her life, so I have a very personal reason for writing this book.

In recent years, I have also seen the effects of paying greater attention to aspects of my own life. Diet and exercise weren't on my agenda in my youth, but I've found that being more attentive to both nowadays has vastly improved my overall physical and mental wellbeing.

Changes don't have to be dramatic, though, to make a difference. A short daily walk, a massage every now and then, incorporating soothing anti-inflammatory foods into your meals... Any healthy adjustments you choose will most likely give you a sense of achievement as well as improving how you feel each day. Whatever alterations you decide on, make sure they're enjoyable!

Understanding Arthritis

What is arthritis?

Arthritis is a condition usually characterized by pain and inflammation in a joint, or joints, anywhere in the body. Its severity ranges from mild to severe.

Although there are numerous different forms of the disease, osteoarthritis (normally resulting from wear and tear on joints), and rheumatoid arthritis (occurring when the body's own immune system attacks joints) are the most common.

When we talk about arthritis, we generally associate it with older adults but it can also occur in childhood & adolescence (juvenile arthritis).

What causes arthritis?

The reasons for developing any form of arthritis vary considerably. Genetics, illness, injury or occupations involving frequently repeated stress on joints may be implicated in triggering some types of arthritis. Yet sometimes the cause is unknown.

Is there any cure?

Whilst there is currently no cure for arthritis, the

intensity of the pain it causes will often fluctuate; sometimes a sufferer will go 'into remission' with symptoms disappearing or lessening for a while with only occasional flare-ups of joint tenderness or stiffness in the morning.

How is it treated?

Depending on the type of arthritis your GP has diagnosed, the aim of treating it will be focused on relief of symptoms and improvement of joint functioning. Some people are prescribed anti-inflammatory drugs and/or physiotherapy. Injections may also be given. In severe cases, surgery to repair, fuse or replace joints can be suggested. It is also reasonable to expect some advice about lifestyle changes.

What about complementary therapies?

Many people seek complementary therapies such as acupuncture, osteopathy, massage and reflexology, to relieve the pain they experience. Interestingly, a significant number notice a marked improvement in both their physical and mental wellbeing as a result. It is advisable, though, to consult your doctor before embarking on any particular form of alternative therapy.

What changes should I make to my lifestyle?

A degree of exercise is extremely important in maintaining joint flexibility. Walking, cycling and swimming are especially beneficial for body and mind when coping with arthritis. Research shows that physical activity not only increases your circulation but also triggers the release of endorphins (the feel-good hormones in your brain), helping you to achieve a positive mindset. Nevertheless, there does need to be a balance. Chronic pain can change from day to day so it is tempting on a 'good day' to overdo things then end up feeling unable to do anything at all for a considerable time afterwards. Doing a moderate amount of exercise daily, interspersed with periods of rest, will maximise its benefits.

Eating a healthy, balanced diet, which includes lots of fruit and vegetables, is essential for everyone to stay well, whether they have arthritis or not. Being overweight puts undue stress on hips, knees, ankles and feet, so keeping your weight within a sensible range for your gender, age and height is especially necessary if you have arthritis.

On the subject of diet, is there anything I should avoid?

There is a great deal of controversy about this. It has been suggested that foods from the nightshade family (such as tomatoes, aubergines, peppers and white potatoes) and citrus fruits (like lemons, grapefruit and oranges) should not be eaten if you have arthritis. However, Arthritis Research UK states that there's absolutely no scientific evidence to support this and actually recommends including them in your diet since they provide much-needed nutrients and antioxidants which have been shown to slow the progression of arthritis.

If you happen to notice, though, that certain fruits and vegetables do increase your pain then obviously they are best avoided.

Foods, containing trans fats such as many ready meals should definitely be eliminated from your diet because, whilst these fats help preserve the food, they contribute to raising bad cholesterol which causes inflammation in the body. So it's wise to avoid buying any product where 'partially hydrogenated oils' is listed in the ingredients on the label.

Research has shown that too much saturated fat (found in produce like meat pies, red meat and cakes) is unhealthy since, besides increasing our risk for a variety of serious illnesses such as heart disease, it can also exacerbate the symptoms of arthritis. Moreover, butter, whole milk and cheese are high in saturated fat so a switch to low-fat dairy products makes good sense.

Refined sugar is another substance to avoid because, as well being high in calories and having no nutritional value, it can also cause inflammation. Adding sweetness to meals is still an option. I sometimes use stevia, which is a non-chemical plant derivative. And pure maple syrup and honey sweeten with the added bonus of being anti-inflammatory.

Do I need to take any supplements?

If you are eating a nutritionally balanced diet, it may be unnecessary to add in supplements. Although you may not eat fish, the omega 3 fatty acids they contain (known to combat inflammation) are present in many of the ingredients listed in the recipes in this book - flax seeds, nuts, kale, broccoli, berries...

However, since the type of arthritis experienced and the particular needs of individuals differ immensely, enlist your doctor's help to decide what is best for you.

What foods can I include in my meals to help soothe arthritis?

According to research, a healthy diet can help reduce the amount of medication required for arthritis and minimize its side effects.

Including anti-inflammatory foods may well help lower both the pain and frequency of flare-ups. So it's a good idea to consume plenty of colourful fruits like blueberries and raspberries and vegetables, particularly leafy green ones such as kale and spinach, to fight inflammation.

Polyunsaturated and monounsaturated fats, found in olive oil, nuts, seeds and avocados, not only lower cholesterol but also have anti-inflammatory properties.

Beans and whole grains - oats, brown rice, wholemeal bread - are all good sources of fibre which keep bowels regular. Additionally, they come into the anti-inflammatory category along with fresh herbs and spices.

I have included all of the above in the recipes that follow.

BREAKFASTS

Index of Breakfasts

Toasted Sourdough with Banana & Cinnamon	11
Blueberry Pancakes	12
Satisfying Almond Shake	13
Tofu Scramble on Toast	14
Warming Oaty Breakfast	16
Peanut Butter Smoothie	17
Ricotta Cheese with Basil & Tomato	18
Strawberry, Nut & Date Treat	19
Lemon & Blueberry Quinoa	20
Tasty Porridge	22
Creamy Scrambled Eggs on Toast	23
Berry Salad with Mixed Spice	24
Apricot & Banana Bagel	25
Lazy Sunday Sweet Potato	26
Poached Eggs on Brioche with Pesto	28
Wholesome Energizing Smoothie	30
Banana & Strawberry Breakfast	32
Overnight Spicy Oats	34
Egg with Avocado on Toast	36
Nourishing Fruit & Nut Smoothie	37

Toasted Sourdough with Banana & Cinnamon

Ingredients

1 thick slice sourdough bread

Almond butter

1 banana, sliced

1 tsp maple syrup

½ tsp cinnamon

Method

- Toast bread
- Place slice onto a serving plate
- Spread almond butter thickly onto toast
- Top with banana slices
- Drizzle maple syrup over
- Sprinkle on cinnamon
- Munch contentedly!

Blueberry Pancakes

Ingredients

1 large egg

112g (4 oz) low-fat yogurt

1-cal olive oil spray

112g (4 oz) pancake mix

112g (4 oz) fresh blueberries

Method

- Whisk egg & yogurt in a bowl
- Stir in pancake mix
- Spray a non-stick pan a few times with oil, & heat
- Spoon in 2 tbsp batter
- Sprinkle a few berries onto pancake
- When edges are firm, turn pancake over & cook for a further minute
- Slide pancake onto a plate and make two more
- Serve the 3 pancakes whilst hot

Satisfying Almond Shake

Ingredients

1 nectarine, de-stoned & sliced

1 tbsp chia seeds

150ml (5 fl.oz) unsweetened almond milk

14g (½ oz) flaked almonds

Pinch of ground cinnamon

1 tsp pure maple syrup

1 tsp oats

½ tsp vanilla extract

Ice cubes

Method

- Put all ingredients into a blender & whizz on high setting
- When the shake is smooth, pour it into a tall glass to drink

Tofu Scramble on Toast

Ingredients

Tiny pinch of sea salt

¼ tsp garlic powder

¼ tsp ground cumin

Tiny pinch of ground chilli

112g (4 oz) extra-firm tofu, crumbled

1 tbsp extra virgin olive oil

¼ red pepper, sliced thinly

2 thin slices red onion

Freshly ground pepper

84g (3 oz) kale, loosely chopped

1 slice wholegrain bread

1 tsp fresh coriander, chopped

Method

- Put salt, garlic powder, cumin & chilli into a small bowl, stir in just sufficient water to make a

pourable liquid & place to one side
- Heat oil in a large lidded frying pan on medium heat
- Stir in red pepper & onion & season with ground pepper
- Cook for approx 4 mins, until softened
- Add kale
- Put lid on & cook for 2 mins
- Add tofu & sauté for 2 mins
- Stir in the seasoned liquid & cook for approx 5 mins until tofu is slightly browned, stirring occasionally
- Meanwhile, toast bread
- Top with scramble & sprinkle coriander over before serving

Warming Oaty Breakfast

Ingredients

240ml (8 fl.oz) semi-skimmed milk

56g (2 oz) oats

1 tsp ground cinnamon

¼ tsp ground cloves

Small pinch each of ground coriander, ground ginger, ground allspice, ground nutmeg & ground cardamom

Stevia, to taste

Method

- Mix all ingredients, except stevia, then cook in a saucepan on medium heat until oats are soft & desired consistency is obtained
- Transfer to serving bowl & add stevia

Peanut Butter Smoothie

Ingredients

168g (6 oz) plain yogurt

2 tbsp peanut butter

1 tbsp chia seeds

Ice cubes

Whole-grain muffin

Method

- Spoon yogurt into a blender
- Add peanut butter & chia seeds
- Drop in ice cubes
- Whizz on high setting until smooth
- Pour into large glass & enjoy with a wholegrain muffin

Ricotta Cheese with Basil & Tomato

Ingredients

2 slices wholegrain bread

2 tbsp ricotta cheese

1 vine tomato, sliced

2 tsp basil

Freshly ground pepper

Method

- Put slices of bread onto a plate & spread 1 tbsp cheese onto each one
- Arrange slices of tomato over both
- Sprinkle each slice with 1 tsp basil
- Season both with pepper - they are ready to enjoy!

Strawberry, Nut & Date Treat

Ingredients

28g (1 oz) shelled Brazil nuts

30 ml (1 fl.oz) water

½ tsp pure vanilla extract

4 large strawberries

4 fresh medjool dates, de-stoned

5 ice cubes

Method

- Put all ingredients into a high powered bullet-style blender, whizz on high setting until smooth
- Spoon into a bowl, serve & relish every tasty mouthful

Lemon & Blueberry Quinoa

Ingredients

56g (2 oz) quinoa

Tiny pinch of salt

120ml (4 fl.oz) unsweetened almond milk

Zest of ¼ lemon

2 tsp maple syrup

56g (2 oz) blueberries

1 tbsp flax seeds

Ground cinnamon to taste

Method

- Put quinoa into a strainer & rinse with cold water until water runs clear
- Pour the milk into a small saucepan & warm it through over medium heat
- Stir quinoa & salt into the milk
- Simmer over medium-low heat until liquid is

absorbed
- Remove saucepan from heat
- Stir lemon zest & maple syrup into the quinoa
- Fold blueberries into mixture
- Transfer to serving bowl then sprinkle with flax seeds & cinnamon

Tasty Porridge

Ingredients

56g (2 oz) porridge oats

Milk, quantity according to instructions on oats packet

½ tsp mixed spice

½ tsp vanilla extract

56g (2 oz) fresh blueberries

56g (2 oz) low-fat cottage cheese

Stevia (to sweeten)

1 tbsp chopped walnuts

Method

- Cook oats according to instructions on packet
- Stir spice & vanilla extract into cooked oats
- Stir in cottage cheese, blueberries & stevia
- Sprinkle with walnuts
- Delicious!

Creamy Scrambled Eggs on Toast

Ingredients

2 eggs

1 tbsp semi skimmed milk

2 tsp olive oil spread

Tiny pinch of salt & pepper

3 tbsp low-fat cottage cheese

1 slice wholegrain toast

Method

- In a blender, whisk eggs with milk & salt & pepper
- Meanwhile, toast bread
- Melt olive oil spread in a non-stick pan, pour in egg mixture, & stir over medium heat
- When eggs are almost ready, stir in cottage cheese
- Top toast with delicious creamy eggs & enjoy!

Berry Salad with Mixed Spice

Ingredients

56g (2 oz) blueberries

6 strawberries, halved

56g (2 oz) blackberries

56g (2 oz) raspberries

56g (2 oz) grapes

A small wedge of melon, cut into small chunks

1 apple, sliced

½ tsp mixed spice

Method

- Put all the fruit into a bowl & mix well
- Sprinkle on the spice
- Hey presto! - it's ready

Apricot & Banana Bagel

Ingredients

1 wholemeal bagel, halved

28g (1 oz) dried (ready to eat) apricots, chopped

28g (1 oz) low fat soft cheese

1 small banana, sliced

¼ tsp cinnamon

Method

- Preheat grill, then toast cut sides of bagel
- Meanwhile mix apricots with soft cheese
- Divide cheese mixture & spread over each bagel half
- Top with banana slices
- Sprinkle with cinnamon
- Savour each delicious mouthful!

Lazy Sunday Sweet Potato

Ingredients

1 sweet potato, sliced

1 tsp extra virgin olive oil

Sea salt & freshly ground pepper, to taste

1 tbsp natural peanut butter

1 small apple

2 tsp pumpkin seeds

1 tsp cinnamon

Method

- Pre-heat oven to 220°C / 425°F / Gas 7
- Coat each potato slice with oil & season with salt & pepper
- Put the slices onto an oiled baking sheet
- Bake for 15 mins
- Turn slices over & bake for a further 15 mins
- Meanwhile peel, core & slice apple

- Transfer potato slices onto your serving plate & spread peanut butter thinly over each one
- Top them with apple slices, seeds & cinnamon

Poached Eggs on Brioche with Pesto

Ingredients

1 brioche bun, halved

28g (1 oz) basil leaves

4 tsp pine nuts

2 tbsp extra virgin olive oil

Freshly ground black pepper

¼ clove garlic

Splash of vinegar

2 large eggs

Method

- Put basil, pine nuts, oil, pepper & garlic in food processor
- Whizz into a smooth purée
- Fill a saucepan with water & add vinegar
- Place pan on medium heat until water is simmering

- Stir water rapidly to swirl then crack an egg & slip it gently into the water
- Repeat with the other egg
- Cook for approx 3 mins until egg whites are just set & eggs still runny
- Meanwhile, toast both halves of brioche
- Spread purée over each one
- Remove eggs from pan using a slotted spoon, place one on each half of brioche & enjoy!

Wholesome Energizing Smoothie

Ingredients

56g (2 oz) spinach

112g (4 oz) frozen pineapple chunks

84g (3 oz) frozen mango chunks

½ medium banana, peeled & sliced

112g (4 oz) cucumber, peeled & chopped

½ tsp fresh ginger, peeled & sliced

3 mint leaves, chopped

¼ tsp ground turmeric

1 tbsp chia seeds

Ice cubes

Method

- Put all ingredients into a blender, except for chia seeds & ice cubes & whizz on high setting until thoroughly combined
- Pour into a tall glass, stir in chia seeds, pop in ice

cubes & sip slowly!

Banana & Strawberry Breakfast

Ingredients

1-cal olive oil spray

1 tbsp ground flax seeds

1 egg

½ small banana, mashed

¼ tsp cinnamon

2 tsp maple syrup

42g (1½ oz) oats

150ml (5 fl oz) unsweetened almond milk

1 tsp vanilla extract

56g (2 oz) strawberries, diced

28g (1 oz) blueberries

Method

- Spray a large, microwave-safe bowl with olive oil cooking spray
- Put in seeds, egg, banana, cinnamon & syrup &

combine thoroughly
- Stir in oats, milk & vanilla extract & mix well
- Microwave on high for approx 2 mins until cooked (time may vary depending on your appliance's wattage)
- Top with strawberries & blueberries & serve

Overnight Spicy Oats

Ingredients

150ml (5 fl.oz) coconut milk

Tip of tsp turmeric

Tip of tsp ginger

Tip of tsp cinnamon

Pinch of black pepper

Pure honey to taste

½ tsp coconut oil

28g (1 oz) porridge oats

1 tbsp chia seeds

84g (3 oz) cherries, de-stoned & halved

4 large strawberries, halved

Method

- Pour milk into a small saucepan, add turmeric, ginger, cinnamon & pepper & whisk until combined completely

- Stir in coconut oil & honey, heat gently & continue stirring until dissolved (without boiling mixture)
- Remove from heat and allow to cool for 10 mins
- Put oats & chia seeds into a jar with lid
- Pour milk mixture into jar, stir well & screw lid on tightly
- Place in fridge overnight
- Scoop out of jar into bowl & serve topped with cherries & strawberries

Egg with Avocado on Toast

Ingredients

½ avocado

1 egg

1 slice of wholegrain bread

Olive oil spread for toast

Handful of fresh spinach leaves

Pinch of red pepper flakes

Method

- Mash avocado
- Toast bread
- Whilst bread is toasting, scramble the egg
- Cover toast with olive oil spread
- Spoon avocado over evenly
- Add spinach leaves
- Top with scrambled egg
- Sprinkle with pepper flakes before enjoying

Nourishing Fruit & Nut Smoothie

Ingredients

56g (2 oz) blueberries

84g (3 oz) strawberries, halved

140g (5 oz) fat-free natural yogurt

3 macadamia nuts

Method

- Put blueberries & strawberries into a blender
- Spoon in yogurt & pop in the nuts
- Blend until completely smooth
- Pour into tall glass & sip slowly

LUNCHES

Index of Lunches

Spicy Kale, Onion & Garlic Omelette	40
Egg with Spinach on Toast	42
Healthy Hummus Roll	44
Tasty Tortilla	45
Spinach Salad with Poppy Seed Dressing	46
Herby Bean Salad	48
Cauliflower Soup	50
Stuffed Red Pepper	52
Tasty Veggie Bun	54
Pesto & Tomato Courgette Spaghetti	56
Black Bean & Kale Wrap	58
Butter Beans with Chilli, Basil & Tomato	60
Pitta & Veggie Batons with Hummus	62
Spicy Vegetable Soup	64
Quick Beetroot, Bean & Lentil Salad	66
Cottage Cheese Wrap	68
Sweet & Savoury Salad	69
Avocado with Egg Healthy	70
Celery Soup Nutty	72
Fruity Smoothie	74

Spicy Kale, Onion & Garlic Omelette

Ingredients

1 tbsp extra virgin olive oil

1 large onion, sliced

½ tsp dried crushed chillies

1 tsp mixed dried herbs

Freshly ground pepper

1 garlic clove, chopped finely

70g (2½ oz) kale

2 large eggs

30ml (1 fl.oz) semi-skimmed milk

Sprig of parsley

Method

- Chop kale into fine strips & rinse
- Heat the olive oil in a non-stick frying pan
- Add the onion, chillies, herbs & pepper & cook gently until onions soften

- Add garlic & cook for a further 2 mins
- Meanwhile, put wet kale strips into a bowl & microwave until just soft, approx 2 mins
- Add kale to pan & stir well
- Whisk eggs with milk, until light & fluffy
- Pour egg mixture into pan, turning heat up to medium
- When eggs begin to set, lower heat & continue to cook until surface of omelette is firm
- Use a spatula to fold one half over & slide omelette onto a plate
- Garnish with parsley & it's ready to eat

Egg with Spinach on Toast

Ingredients

2 tsp extra virgin olive oil

1 large handful baby spinach

1 slice whole-grain bread

2 medium eggs

2 tbsp milk

Freshly ground pepper to taste

Sprig of parsley

Method

- Heat oil in frying pan over medium heat
- Add spinach & cook, stirring frequently until spinach wilts
- Meanwhile, toast bread
- Whisk eggs with milk & pepper
- Stir egg mixture into spinach
- Continue stirring until eggs are cooked

- Place toast on a plate & spoon egg mixture onto it
- Garnish with parsley & enjoy

Healthy Hummus Roll

Ingredients

Large wholegrain roll

2 tbsp hummus

1 small tomato, sliced

¼ cucumber, peeled & sliced

½ carrot, grated

4 black olives, halved

1 tbsp alfalfa sprouts

Method

- Slice roll in half
- Spread hummus over one half
- Arrange tomato & cucumber on top of it
- Add carrot
- Top with olives & alfalfa sprouts
- Cover with other half of roll & tuck in!

Tasty Tortilla

Ingredients

Small can black beans

2 tbsp salsa

¼ tsp ground cumin

1 egg

1 corn tortilla

1 tbsp reduced fat grated cheese

Method

- Pour the black beans & their juice into a small pan
- Add cumin & salsa & heat through
- Cook the egg whichever way you prefer
- Toast corn tortilla lightly
- Place tortilla on a plate
- Top with beans & egg
- Sprinkle cheese over & enjoy each mouthful

Spinach Salad with Poppy Seed Dressing

Salad Ingredients

28g (1 oz) baby spinach

3 large ripe strawberries, sliced

2 tbsp crumbled feta cheese

3 tbsp chopped walnuts

Dressing Ingredients

3 large ripe strawberries, chopped

¼ tsp mild onion, finely chopped

2 tsp apple cider vinegar

Salt & freshly ground pepper to taste

¾ tsp poppy seeds

1 tbsp extra virgin olive oil

Wholemeal roll

Method

Salad:
- Place strawberries in a bowl
- Stir in the spinach, feta & walnuts

Dressing:
- Put strawberries in a blender
- Add onion vinegar, salt & pepper
- Blend on high setting until smooth
- Transfer contents to a cup & stir in poppy seeds & oil
- Pour dressing over salad, toss & transfer to a plate
- Serve with wholemeal roll

Herby Bean Salad

Ingredients

224g (8 oz) of canned white beans, drained & rinsed

2 sun-dried tomatoes, sliced

½ red pepper, chopped

1 small red onion, chopped

2 tsp fresh parsley, chopped

2 tsp coriander, chopped

4 tsp extra virgin olive oil

½ tbsp lemon juice

Freshly ground pepper

1 slice wholegrain bread

Method

- Toast bread & cut in half
- Put beans, tomatoes, red pepper, onion, parsley & coriander into a bowl
- Add oil, lemon juice & ground pepper

- Toss well to mix
- Place bowl in centre of a plate & put toast on each side of it
- Eat slowly, savouring the different flavours

Cauliflower Soup

Ingredients

240ml (8 fl oz) vegetable stock

1 tbsp lemon juice

½ medium cauliflower, broken up into florets

2 tsp extra virgin olive oil

1 small spring onion, chopped

Pinch of ground nutmeg

Pinch of ground black pepper

Sprig parsley

Method

- Pour stock into a saucepan, add lemon juice & bring to the boil
- Lower heat to medium, put cauliflower into stock & cook until tender, approx 10 mins, then remove from heat without draining off liquid
- Warm oil in non-stick frying pan, add spring onion

& cook for approx 5 mins, until tender
- Pour cauliflower, with its stock, into a blender & add spring onions
- Blend until smooth
- Transfer to serving bowl
- Stir in nutmeg & pepper
- Garnish with parsley

Stuffed Red Pepper

Ingredients

1 medium-sized red pepper, halved lengthways & de-seeded

56g (2 oz) couscous

90ml (3 fl oz) boiling water

1-cal olive oil spray

1 small onion, chopped

Juice & zest of ½ lemon

½ tsp ground coriander

1 dried apricot, chopped

28g (1 oz) feta cheese, crumbled

Method

- Preheat oven to 200°C / 400°F / Gas 6
- Put pepper halves on oiled or non-stick baking tray & cook for 10 mins until tender
- While it's cooking put the couscous into a bowl,

pour boiling water over, cover & put to one side for 10 mins until water is absorbed
- Spray small frying pan with oil to coat, heat gently & fry onion until soft
- Fluff couscous up with a fork
- Add to couscous onion, lemon juice & zest, coriander, apricot & feta cheese
- Fill roasted peppers with couscous mixture & serve

Tasty Veggie Bun

Ingredients

2 tsp extra virgin olive oil

2 slices aubergine

2 slices red onion

½ courgette, sliced

½ small red pepper, de-seeded & sliced

½ tsp fresh thyme

Freshly ground pepper

1 small vine tomato, sliced

½ tsp red wine vinegar

4 leaves basil, torn

1 tbsp hummus

1 ciabatta bun, halved

A few rocket leaves

Method

- Preheat oven to 200°C / 400°F / Gas 6

- In a bowl, mix oil thoroughly into aubergine, onion, courgette, red pepper & thyme & season with ground pepper
- Transfer to non-stick baking sheet & roast in oven until softened & beginning to char (approx 15 mins)
- Toast ciabatta bun halves
- Toss tomato with vinegar & basil
- Spread hummus over bun base
- Place rocket onto hummus, pile on roasted vegetables, top with tomato & cover with other half of bun
- It's ready to eat!

Pesto & Tomato Courgette Spaghetti

Ingredients

1 tsp extra virgin olive oil

5 plum tomatoes, halved

1 tbsp balsamic vinegar

½ garlic clove, crushed

Freshly ground pepper

1 large courgette, spiralised or very thinly sliced into narrow strips

2 tbsp vegetarian pesto

1 tbsp toasted pine nuts

Method

- In a bowl, mix oil thoroughly with tomatoes, vinegar, garlic & pepper
- Spoon into frying pan & cook for approx 5 mins, stirring frequently
- Put courgette spaghetti into a bowl & cover with

boiling water to blanch for 30 seconds
- Drain well
- Stir in pesto until spaghetti is completely coated & season with pepper
- Add tomatoes & sprinkle on pine nuts before serving

Black Bean & Kale Wrap

Ingredients

2 medium kale leaves

2 tsp fresh lime juice

1 tsp coriander, chopped

2 tsp extra virgin olive oil

Pinch of chilli powder

Pinch of ground cumin

Pinch of sea salt

112g (4 oz) canned black beans, rinsed and drained

1 clove garlic, minced

2 tbsp water

1 small (8 inch) whole wheat tortilla

½ small avocado, de-stoned & sliced into thin strips

1 tbsp red onion, chopped

2 tbsp feta cheese, crumbled

Method

- Wash & dry kale, remove stems & chop leaves into small pieces
- In a bowl, mix kale, lime juice, coriander, 1 tsp olive oil, cumin, chilli powder & sea salt, then put to one side to marinate
- In a small saucepan, heat 1 tsp of olive oil & sauté garlic
- Add beans & water & heat gently
- Mash beans & add salt to taste
- Warm tortilla in the microwave for approx 15 seconds
- Spoon black bean mixture onto tortilla & top with sliced avocado & half the marinated kale
- Add red onion & feta cheese
- Roll up tortilla, folding in the sides
- Slice in half & serve with remainder of marinated kale

Butter Beans with Chilli, Basil & Tomato

Ingredients

3 tbsp of extra virgin olive oil

1 red onion, chopped

1 clove of garlic, crushed

1 small chilli, chopped

1 small can of butter beans, drained & chopped

1 small can of chopped tomatoes

2 tbsp basil, chopped

250ml (8 fl.oz) of water

Freshly ground pepper to taste

2 slices wholegrain bread, toasted

Method

- Put 1 tbsp oil into a non-stick pan & heat gently
- Cook onion, garlic & chilli until onions begin to brown
- Add beans, tomatoes & basil & stir well

- Season with pepper
- Add half the water & bring to the boil, then turn down to simmer on a low heat
- Cook, stirring occasionally, adding more water as required to prevent mixture becoming too dry, until beans are warmed through
- Meanwhile, drizzle each bread slice with 1 tbsp oil & grill until crispy
- Place toast on a serving plate, top both slices with the mixture & enjoy!

Pitta & Veggie Batons with Hummus

Ingredients

2 tbsp canned chickpeas

1 tbsp low-fat natural yogurt

1 tbsp extra virgin olive oil

Juice of ½ lemon

¼ tsp ground cumin

¼ tsp paprika

1 clove of garlic, chopped finely

1 wholemeal pitta bread, sliced into sticks

1 stick of celery, sliced into batons

1 carrot, sliced into batons

Method

- Drain chickpeas then put them, together with yogurt, oil, lemon juice, cumin, paprika & garlic, into a bowl
- Use a blender to combine thoroughly until it

forms a smooth hummus
- Arrange pitta bread sticks & veggie batons on side of a plate with bowl of hummus in the centre
- Dip to your heart's content!

Spicy Vegetable Soup

Ingredients

2 carrots, peeled & chopped

1 small onion, chopped

½ parsnip, peeled & chopped

1 garlic clove, crushed

1 tsp virgin coconut oil

Small pinch of cayenne pepper

½ tsp turmeric powder

360ml (12 fl.oz) low sodium vegetable broth

Juice of ¼ lemon

Small piece of fresh ginger, peeled & grated

1 tbsp natural yogurt

Sprig of parsley

Method

- Preheat oven to 180°C / 350°F / Gas 4
- Line a baking sheet with greaseproof paper

- Put onto it carrots, onion, parsnip & garlic
- Sprinkle turmeric & cayenne pepper over vegetables
- Drizzle coconut oil over & mix in until evenly coated
- Roast mixture for 15 mins
- Meanwhile, heat vegetable broth & allow to cool slightly for approx 5 mins
- Transfer veggie mixture to blender
- Add in vegetable broth, then lemon juice & ginger
- Blend until completely smooth
- Pour into a serving bowl
- Drizzle yogurt over, garnish with parsley & serve whilst warm

Quick Beetroot, Bean & Lentil Salad

Ingredients

84g (3 oz) baby beetroots, sliced

112g (4 oz) green beans, trimmed & sliced

1 tbsp chopped mint

84g (3 oz) baby spinach leaves

56g (2 oz) rocket

½ small avocado, diced

112g (4 oz) canned lentils, drained

2 tsp extra virgin olive oil

2 tsp balsamic vinegar

Freshly ground black pepper

1 tbsp pumpkin seeds

Method

- Put all above ingredients, apart from pumpkin seeds, into a large bowl
- Mix well until thoroughly combined

- Sprinkle pumpkin seeds over & enjoy

Cottage Cheese Wrap

Ingredients

¼ cucumber, peeled & finely chopped

28g (1 oz) cottage cheese

Freshly ground pepper

1 wholewheat tortilla

Sprig of watercress

Couple of crisp lettuce leaves, shredded

1 tsp lemon juice

Freshly ground black pepper

Method

- In a bowl, mix cucumber & cheese together & season with pepper
- Place tortilla on a plate & spread mixture onto it
- Add watercress & lettuce
- Drizzle lemon juice over before rolling up & cutting in half

Sweet & Savoury Salad

Ingredients

2 curly kale leaves

½ avocado

½ mango

2 asparagus spears

56g (2 oz) raisins

28g (1 oz) toasted seeds of your choice

28g (2 oz) cooked red kidney beans

Method

- Tear kale leaves into strips
- Dice avocado & mango & slice asparagus spears lengthways
- Combine with raisins, seeds & beans in a bowl, toss & serve

Avocado with Egg

Ingredients

½ avocado

1 egg

¼ cucumber

Freshly ground pepper

Mixed salad of your choice

Vinaigrette

2 tsp rice wine vinegar

¼ tsp honey

½ tsp sesame oil

2 tsp chopped dill

Method

- Preheat oven to 220°C / 425°F / Gas 7
- Remove a small amount of the flesh from the avocado to make a bigger hole for the egg to go in

(You can eat this now!)
- Put the avocado into an ovenproof dish & crack egg into the middle of it
- Bake for approx 15 mins, until egg is set
- While it is cooking, make the vinaigrette by mixing vinegar, honey, sesame oil & 1 tsp of dill in a bowl
- Slice cucumber into thin strips using potato peeler
- Stir strips into the dressing, coating thoroughly
- Put mixed salad on one side of a serving plate
- Place baked avocado beside it & sprinkle with rest of the dill
- Season with pepper
- Spoon cucumber strips onto the plate
- Dress salad with vinaigrette to complete this delicious meal

Celery Soup

Ingredients

1 tbsp extra virgin olive oil

140g (5 oz) celery, chopped

½ red onion, chopped

1 garlic clove, chopped

210ml (7 fl.oz) hot vegetable stock

1 slice ciabatta

Method

- Heat oil in a saucepan
- Put in the celery, onion & garlic & cook on a low heat for approx 5 mins, until softened
- Add vegetable stock & simmer gently for 10 mins
- Allow to cool for approx 5 mins
- Meanwhile, toast ciabatta
- Pour cooled soup into a blender & blend on high setting

- Transfer soup into a bowl & serve with ciabatta

Nutty, Fruity Smoothie

Ingredients

1 small banana

1 peach

14g (½ oz) walnuts

1 tbsp oats

1 tsp vanilla extract

120ml (4 fl.oz) unsweetened almond milk

1 tsp pure maple syrup

Pinch of ground cinnamon

Couple of ice cubes

Method

- Put all ingredients into a blender and blitz on high setting until completely until smooth
- Pour into large serving glass

DINNERS

Index of dinners

Tuscan Roasted Vegetable Salad	77
Baked Potato with Avocado & Feta	79
Broccoli with Mushroom, Cashews & Noodles	82
Roasted Veggies with Pasta	84
Warming Stir Fry with Rice	86
Tasty Cheesy Macaroni	88
Baked Potato with Bulgur Wheat & Vegetables	90
Lentil & Cauliflower Curry	92
Chickpea & Oat Dumplings in Tomato Sauce	94
Quorn & Vegetable Stew	96
Spaghetti with Tofu	98
Quinoa Ratatouille	100
Vegetable Curry	102
Savoury Ginger Stir Fry	104
Chillied Beans & Pumpkin	106
Butternut Squash & Pea Risotto	108
Curried Chickpeas with Rice	110
Courgette & Mushroom Risotto	112
Quinoa Pilaf with Spinach & Cheese	114
Baked Sweet Potato with Beans & Slaw	116

Tuscan Roasted Vegetable Salad

Ingredients

224g (8 oz) wholemeal bread, cut into chunky cubes

3 tbsp extra virgin olive oil

2 sprigs rosemary, stems removed

Sea salt

Freshly ground black pepper

28g (1 oz) whole hazelnuts

1 small garlic clove, crushed

1 tsp pure maple syrup

1 tsp lemon juice

56g (2 oz) radishes, chopped

84g (3 oz) chopped Brussels sprouts, chopped

1 tbsp chopped shallot

1 small carrot, chopped

168g (6 oz) sweet potatoes, peeled & sliced thinly

¼ beetroot, thinly sliced

112g (4 oz) spinach leaves

1 tbsp pomegranate seeds

Method

- Preheat oven to 180°C / 350°F / Gas 4
- Put bread cubes in a bowl & coat well with 1 tbsp oil
- Add leaves of 1 sprig of rosemary & season with salt & pepper
- Line a baking tray with a greaseproof paper
- Spread contents of bowl & nuts onto it
- Toast in oven for 10 mins then remove
- In a bowl, whisk 2 tbsp olive oil, crushed garlic pinch of pepper, maple syrup, lemon juice & leaves of remaining sprig of rosemary
- In another bowl, put radishes, Brussels sprouts, shallot, carrot, potatoes & beetroot
- Combine the contents of both bowls & toss together
- Lay your vegetables flat on a lined baking sheet or roasting pan
- Place in oven

- After 10 mins, turn the vegetables & continue cooking for 8-10 more mins or until vegetables are cooked (checking & turning occasionally)
- Put spinach leaves into serving bowl & add roasted vegetables, toasted bread & hazelnuts
- Toss well
- Garnish with pomegranate seeds

Baked Potato with Avocado & Feta

Ingredients

1 large sweet potato

1 tsp olive oil

Pinch of sea salt

Pinch of ground black pepper

1 small ripe avocado

Juice of ½ fresh lime

28g (1 oz) pumpkin seeds

42g (1½ oz) Greek feta cheese

1 tsp chipotle salsa

Method

- Preheat oven to 180ºC / 350°F / Gas 4
- Drizzle oil over potato, sprinkle with sea salt & black pepper
- Wrap in foil & bake in the oven for approx 1 hour, until tender

- Shortly before potato is cooked, de-stone & chop avocados & mix with lime juice
- Toast pumpkin seeds in dry pan for few mins until beginning to turn golden
- Unwrap potato & slice in half
- Top with avocado, crumble over the cheese & sprinkle toasted seeds on top
- Drizzle chipotle salsa over before serving

Broccoli with Mushroom, Cashews & Noodles

Ingredients

1 vegetable stock cube

1 nest medium egg noodles

Florets of ½ small head broccoli

2 tsp sesame oil

140g (5 oz) chestnut mushrooms, cut into thick slices

2 spring onions, sliced finely

1 small garlic clove, chopped finely

Tip of tsp chilli flakes

1 tbsp hoisin sauce

28g (1 oz) roasted cashew nuts

Method

- Put stock cube into a pan of water & bring to the boil
- Drop in noodle nest, bring back to boil & cook for 2 mins

- Pop in broccoli & cook for 2 further mins
- Pour 120 ml (4oz) of stock into a cup & put to one side
- Drain broccoli & noodles
- Heat a wok & add sesame oil
- Put in mushrooms & stir fry for 2 mins until starting to become golden
- Stir in ¾ of the spring onions
- Add garlic & chilli flakes & cook for 1 more min
- Add noodles & broccoli
- Stir in 2 tbsp of stock
- Add hoisin sauce & toss thoroughly
- Transfer contents of wok to serving plate
- Sprinkle rest of spring onions & cashew nuts over to complete this healthy meal

Roasted Veggies with Pasta

Ingredients

1 onion, sliced into wedges

1 red pepper, sliced into chunks

1 courgette, sliced into chunks

112g (4 oz) mushrooms

¼ tsp minced garlic

2 tsp extra virgin olive oil

Freshly ground pepper & sea salt, to taste

84g (3oz) wholewheat pasta

Method

- Preheat oven to 220°C / 425°F / Gas 7
- In a bowl, mix onion, peppers, courgette, mushrooms & garlic with oil, salt & pepper
- Transfer to an oven tray lined with foil, spread out evenly
- Roast for approx 15 mins, until tender

- While the veggies are roasting, cook pasta according to instructions on packet
- Rinse pasta with boiling water & drain
- Tip pasta into serving bowl & stir in veggie mix
- Delicious!

Warming Stir Fry with Rice

Ingredients

84g (3oz) brown rice

150g (5 oz) potatoes, peeled & halved

2 tsps extra virgin olive oil

1 small onion, diced

¼ tsp cumin seeds

¼ tsp black mustard seeds

½ small fresh green chilli, de-seeded & sliced thinly

¼ pointed cabbage, shredded

Tiny pinch of sea salt

1 tbsp chopped coriander

1 tsp lemon juice

2 tsp toasted coconut shavings

Method

- Put rice on to cook, according to instructions on packet

- Meanwhile, cook potatoes in a saucepan of salted boiling water for approx 10 mins
- Drain rice & potatoes & return to their pans
- Cover rice with lid & put to one side
- Lightly break potatoes into smaller pieces
- Heat oil gently in frying pan, add onion, cumin, mustard seeds & chilli & cook for a few mins until chilli begins to turn dark
- Add cabbage & salt & stir-fry for 3mins
- Add potatoes to the pan & cook for approx 2 mins until the cabbage is tender but still slightly crunchy
- Stir in coriander, lemon juice & coconut serve with the cooked rice

Tasty Cheesy Macaroni

Ingredients

56g (2 oz) macaroni, uncooked

1 tbsp cornflour

100ml (3½ fl.oz) skimmed milk

28g (1 oz) reduced fat cheddar cheese, grated

½ tsp mustard

Sea salt & freshly ground pepper, to taste

Sprig of parsley

Handful of rocket

Method

- Cook macaroni according to instructions on packet
- Whilst it's cooking, in a saucepan mix the cornflour with 2 tbsp of the milk to a smooth consistency
- Gradually add the rest of the milk & bring to the

boil slowly, stirring continuously until mixture thickens
- Mix in cheese, mustard, salt & pepper
- Gently stir in the cooked pasta
- Spoon mixture onto a plate & garnish with parsley
- Add rocket & serve

Baked Potato with Bulgur Wheat & Vegetables

Ingredients

1 sweet potato

2 tbsp extra virgin olive oil

Small pinch of sea salt

½ red pepper, chopped

6 cherry tomatoes

½ fennel bulb, thinly sliced

½ red onion, cut into wedges

56g (2oz) bulgur wheat

3 sprigs of dill, roughly chopped

Freshly ground black pepper

3 tbsp natural yogurt

Method

- Preheat oven to 200C / 400°F / Gas 6
- Rub potato with ½ tsp of the olive oil & salt
- Use a sharp knife to pierce potato several times,

- Put potato onto lightly oiled foil in oven for 1 hr
- Put peppers, tomatoes, fennel & onion into a roasting tray
- Drizzle rest of oil over & mix thoroughly
- Sprinkle with ground pepper & cook for approx 20 mins, until softened & browning at the edge of veggies
- Meanwhile, tip bulgur wheat into heatproof bowl & pour in sufficient boiling water to just cover bulgur wheat
- Cover bowl & let it stand for ½ hr to absorb water
- Check potato is cooked by testing with a knifepoint
- Fluff bulgur wheat with a fork
- Put in the roasted vegetables & dill & mix well
- Cut potato lengthways in half on a serving plate
- Spoon bulgur wheat & vegetables onto each half
- Top each one with yogurt & enjoy!

Lentil & Cauliflower Curry

Ingredients

2 tbsp extra virgin olive oil

2 cloves garlic, crushed

½ small onion, chopped

56g (2 oz) uncooked red lentils, rinsed

480 ml (16 fl.oz) hot vegetable stock

400g (14oz) can chopped tomatoes

¼ tsp cayenne pepper

1 tsp curry powder

1 tsp cumin

140g (5 oz) frozen cauliflower florets

Method

- Heat olive oil in a large saucepan on medium heat
- Add garlic & onion & cook for 2 mins
- Stir in lentils & stock & heat until simmering
- Cover saucepan & cook for approx 45 mins, until

lentils have softened, stirring occasionally (add in water if contents get too dry)
- Add tomatoes, cayenne pepper, curry powder, cumin & cauliflower & cook for further 10 mins before spooning onto serving plate

Chickpea & Oat Dumplings in Tomato Sauce

Ingredients

6 tbsp extra virgin olive oil

1 small onion, chopped

½ tsp ground cumin

7g (¼ oz) coriander leaves

100g (3½ oz) canned chickpeas, drained

Freshly ground black pepper

28g (1 oz) oats

150 ml (5 fl.oz) passata with onion & garlic

45 ml (1½ fl.oz) water

84g (3 oz) frozen sliced green beans

1 medium carrot, peeled & sliced

Sprig of parsley

Method

- Heat 2 tbsp oil in small frying pan
- Stir in onion & cook until softened, approx 3 mins

- Add cumin & cook for 1 min more, stirring continuously
- Spoon into a bullet-style blender, add coriander, chickpeas, 2 tbsp oil & season with pepper
- Blend to coarse purée
- Transfer to a bowl & stir in oats
- Put the carrots & beans onto cook (steaming them is particularly healthy)
- Use your hands to form 4 small balls (dumplings) out of the mixture
- Heat remaining oil in frying pan (the one used for the onions)
- Fry dumplings gently for approx 4 mins, until an even golden brown, turning frequently
- Pour in water & passata
- Bring to boil & simmer for approx 2 mins, stirring occasionally
- Spoon onto a plate & serve with the beans & carrots

Quorn & Vegetable Stew

Ingredients

2 tbsp extra virgin olive oil

½ onion, sliced thinly

1 green pepper, sliced thinly

56g (2 oz) Quorn pieces

½ clove garlic, chopped

½ tsp paprika

200g (7 oz) canned chopped tomatoes with their juice

½ tsp dried oregano

½ tsp tomato purée

60ml (2 fl.oz) red wine

Sea salt

Ground black pepper

Sprig of parsley

Method

- Heat oil in a frying pan & cook onion until tender

- Add green pepper & Quorn & cook for further 5 mins, until pepper is tender, stirring continuously
- Stir in garlic & paprika
- Tip in tomatoes & juice & stir
- Stir in oregano & tomato purée
- Pour in wine & stir again
- Bring mixture to the boil
- Lower heat, cover & simmer for 20 mins, stirring occasionally
- Once liquid thickens, stir in salt & pepper
- Ladle onto serving plate & garnish with sprig of parsley

Spaghetti with Tofu

Ingredients

70g (2½ oz) wholewheat spaghetti

Olive oil spray

1 tsp sesame oil

2 garlic cloves, crushed

Thumb-size piece fresh ginger, peeled & chopped

120ml (4 fl oz) vegetable stock

2 tbsp teriyaki sauce

½ tbsp cornflour

56g (2 oz) tofu, drained

56g (2 oz) mangetout

28g (1 oz) canned water chestnuts, drained & chopped

84g (3 oz) mushrooms, sliced

Small wedge of iceberg lettuce, torn

Method

- Put spaghetti on to cook according to instructions

- on packet
- Meanwhile, coat a large saucepan with olive oil spray & heat sesame oil on low heat
- Add garlic & ginger & cook for 3 mins
- Add 60ml (2 fl oz) of vegetable stock & teriyaki sauce & cook for 5 mins
- Combine rest of stock in a bowl with cornflour, stir until smooth & add to teriyaki mixture, simmering for approx 3 mins (until sauce is thickened)
- Add tofu, mangetout, water chestnuts & mushrooms to sauce & cook for approx 3 more mins
- Drain spaghetti & rinse with boiling water (to take out excess starch)
- Stir spaghetti into sauce mixture
- Serve with lettuce to complete your tasty meal

Quinoa Ratatouille

Ingredients

75g (2½ oz) packet pre-soaked quinoa

150ml (5 fl.oz) vegetable stock

4 tsp olive oil

1 small onion, sliced finely

½ tsp dried mixed herbs

1 small clove garlic, crushed

2 small celery stalks, chopped

1 small red pepper, diced

1 small courgette, diced

¼ tsp chilli powder

200g (7 oz) can of chopped tomatoes

Method

- Rinse quinoa thoroughly
- Pour vegetable stock into a saucepan & bring to the boil

- Add quinoa & cook on low heat until it is softened & liquid is absorbed, approx 15 mins
- While it's cooking, heat olive oil in a non-stick frying pan
- Fry onions with herbs & garlic until onions start to soften
- Add celery & cook until it begins to soften
- Add red pepper & courgette & cook for 2 further mins
- Add chilli powder & tomatoes
- Cover pan & simmer on low heat for approx 10 mins
- Transfer quinoa to a serving bowl
- Spoon ratatouille over & eat while hot

Vegetable Curry

Ingredients

Florets from 1 small head of broccoli

2 tsp coconut oil

1 small garlic clove, minced

¼ tsp cumin

¼ tsp coriander

¼ tsp turmeric

Pinch of chilli powder

¼ tsp sea salt

180ml (6 fl.oz) coconut milk

1 small red pepper, de-seeded & chopped

1 large carrot, chopped

112g (4 oz) frozen peas

Fresh herbs of your choice for garnish

2 poppadoms

Method

- Roughly chop florets
- Put coconut oil, garlic, spices & sea salt into a medium sized saucepan & stir
- Pour in coconut milk & stir
- Add in the broccoli, red pepper & carrot & stir again
- Bring mixture to a boil
- Cover saucepan with a lid, reduce heat & simmer contents for 6 mins
- Add in the peas, stir thoroughly until simmering again
- Cook for a further 5-8 mins until broccoli & carrots are tender
- Serve in a bowl garnished with the fresh herbs of your choice
- Enjoy with poppadoms

Savoury Ginger Stir Fry

Ingredients

2 wholewheat noodle nests

½ tsp miso paste dissolved in 1 tbsp boiling water

2 tsp tomato purée

14g (½ oz) peeled root ginger, grated

1 tbsp extra virgin olive oil

1 tbsp sesame oil

½ green pepper, sliced into thin strips

½ red pepper, sliced into thin strips

Small wedge white cabbage, sliced thinly

28g (1 oz) edamame beans

½ carrot, peeled & sliced into thin strips

½ red chilli, chopped finely

3 spring onions, chopped

28g (1 oz) cashews, roughly chopped

Method

- In a bowl mix tomato purée & warm miso
- Put grated ginger in centre of piece of paper towelling, scrunch it up & squeeze juice into miso mixture
- Cook noodles, according to instructions on packet, drain, cover & put to one side
- Heat both oils together in a wok & stir fry peppers, cabbage, beans, carrot, chilli, spring onion & nuts for 4 mins
- Stir in the ginger & miso mix & cook for 1 more min
- Spoon noodles onto serving plate, top with contents of wok & bring your taste buds to life with each delicious mouthful!

Chillied Beans & Pumpkin

Ingredients

168g (6 oz) of pumpkin, de-seeded & cut into cubes

200g (7 oz) canned red kidney beans, drained

2 tsp dried oregano

200g (7 oz) canned chopped tomatoes

2 tsp ground cinnamon

1 tsp ground chilli

120ml (4 fl.oz) water

1 tsp cornflour

1 tbsp water

1 wholewheat tortilla

Method

- Preheat the oven to 200°C / 400°F / Gas Mark 6
- Steam-cook pumpkin until it can be pieced with a knife, approx 15 mins
- Put pumpkin, beans, oregano, tomatoes,

cinnamon, chilli & 120ml water into a casserole
- Cover with lid & bake in oven for 20 mins
- Mix 1 tbsp water with the cornflour, stir into casserole mixture & cook for approx 15 more mins
- When it's cooked, serve with the tortilla

Butternut Squash & Pea Risotto

Ingredients

4 tbsp olive oil

1 small clove garlic, chopped finely

1 small onion, chopped finely

½ tsp dried mixed herbs

75g (2½ oz) brown rice

112g (4 oz) butternut squash, peeled & diced

½ litre (17 fl.oz) vegetable stock

1 tsp apple cider vinegar

1 tsp lemon juice

2 tsp low salt soy sauce

112g (4 oz) peas

Method

- Heat 1 tbsp of olive oil a large saucepan
- Put in garlic, onion & mixed herbs & cook until just softened

- Stir in rice & cook for 3 mins
- Stir in vinegar, lemon juice & soy sauce & gradually add about half the stock, on a low heat (to prevent mixture drying out too quickly)
- Cook until liquid is absorbed
- Meanwhile heat remaining 3 tbsp oil in another pan
- Add squash & cook until it starts to brown
- Stir squash, peas & remaining stock into rice mixture
- Cook until rice is softened but not mushy, adding in water as necessary to prevent mixture drying out
- Remove from heat, cover pan with a lid & leave for approx 8 mins before spooning onto serving plate

Curried Chickpeas with Rice

Ingredients

112g (4 oz) basmati rice

1 tsp extra virgin olive oil

½ onion, diced finely

½ tsp fresh ginger, chopped finely

1 clove garlic, chopped finely

¼ tsp dried crushed chillies

1 tsp curry powder

180ml (6 fl.oz) coconut milk

120ml (4 fl.oz) vegetable broth

½ tsp honey

1 small can of chickpeas, drained & rinsed

Couple of coriander leaves

Method

- Cook rice according to the instructions on the packet

- Heat oil in a small frying pan on medium heat
- Add onions & ginger & cook for approx 3 mins, until onions are softened
- Stir in garlic, curry powder & chillies & continue cooking for 2 mins
- Pour in coconut milk & broth
- Stir in honey & bring to the boil
- Mix in chickpeas & simmer on low heat for 8 mins
- Pile rice in centre of serving dish
- Spoon chickpea mixture over rice
- Garnish with coriander

Courgette & Mushroom Risotto

Ingredients

56g (2 oz) courgette, diced

112g (4 oz) mushrooms, cleaned & diced

2 tbsp extra virgin olive oil

1 additional tsp olive oil

Sea salt & freshly ground pepper

1 small onion, chopped finely

84g (3 oz) long grain brown rice, uncooked

1 tbsp white wine

240ml (8 fl.oz) vegetable broth

1 small garlic clove, chopped finely

1 tbsp parsley, chopped finely

28g (1 oz) parmesan-style cheese, grated

Handful of rocket

Method

- In a saucepan, gently heat 1 tbsp oil

- Put in courgette, mushrooms & a little salt & pepper
- Cook, stirring continuously until they soften
- Scoop onto a plate & put to one side
- In the same saucepan, heat another tbsp oil & sauté onion, until translucent
- Add rice & continue cooking, whilst stirring for approx 3 mins
- Stir in the wine & cook until wine evaporates
- Pour in half of the broth & cook on medium heat until most of it evaporates, stirring occasionally
- Pour in rest of the broth & cook until it has been absorbed & rice is nearly done (adding a little water if necessary)
- Stir in courgette, mushrooms, parsley & garlic & 1 tsp oil
- Spoon onto a serving plate & sprinkle with cheese
- Garnish by scattering rocket liberally over the risotto

Quinoa Pilaf with Spinach & Cheese

Ingredients

40g (1½ oz) quinoa

200ml (7 fl.oz) boiling water

3 tbsp extra virgin olive oil

2 tbsp sunflower seeds

1 large clove garlic, chopped finely

56g (2 oz) spinach leaves, chopped

42g (1½ oz) cheddar cheese, grated

2 tsp lemon juice

Method

- Rinse quinoa thoroughly
- Put into saucepan & add boiling water
- Bring to boil, reduce heat, cover & simmer for approx 15 mins, until water is absorbed & quinoa tender
- Fluff with fork & put to one side

- Heat the olive oil in frying pan on medium heat
- Add sunflower seeds & lightly toast, approx 2 mins
- Add garlic & cook until it softens, approx 2 mins
- Stir in spinach & quinoa & cook stirring continuously until the quinoa is hot & spinach wilts
- Add nearly all the cheese & the lemon juice & stir until cheese melts
- Ladle onto serving plate & sprinkle with rest of the cheese

Baked Sweet Potato with Beans & Slaw

Ingredients

1 medium sweet potato, washed & dried

2 tbsp olive oil

Pinch of sea salt

½ small onion, finely chopped

1 garlic clove, finely chopped

Pinch of crushed chillies

1 tsp cumin seeds

400g (7 oz) tin black beans, drained

100ml (3½ fl oz) vegetable stock

28g (1 oz) reduced fat cheddar cheese, grated

For the Slaw

¼ small red cabbage, thinly sliced

½ red onion, sliced thinly

5 radishes, sliced thinly

Juice of ½ lime

2 sprigs coriander, chopped

Sea salt & freshly ground pepper

Method

- Preheat oven to 200°C /400°F / Gas 6
- Coat potato with ½ tsp of oil & pinch of salt
- Pierce potato skin in several places & put on oiled foil on top shelf of oven for approx 1 hr
- Meanwhile, put all ingredients for the slaw into a bowl, mix well & put to one side
- When potato is almost done, heat rest of oil in a small saucepan on medium heat & fry onion & garlic for approx 2 mins, until onion softens
- Add chillies & cumin & fry for 1-2 mins, until fragrant & soft
- Add beans & stock & simmer on low heat until liquid evaporates & beans are soft
- When potato is cooked through (pierce with a knife to check) turn oven off & leave the potato in until bean mix is cooked
- Cut potato in half on a serving plate & use a fork

to fluff up flesh

- Top each half with beans & sprinkle with cheese
- Spoon slaw onto side of plate & relish slowly

Printed in Poland
by Amazon Fulfillment
Poland Sp. z o.o., Wrocław